9 Lively Cat Tales
and Other Pet Poems

To find more books by Jeffry Glover
please visit his website at *www.JeffryGlover.com*

9 Lively Cat Tales
and Other Pet Poems

Jeffry Glover

POEMS FOR PLEASURE PRESS
Stoughton, Wisconsin

© 2019 Jeffry Glover. All rights reserved. No part of this work may be reproduced, transmitted, or distributed by any means, electronic or mechanical, without the express written permission of the author except for brief excerpts, which may be quoted in reviews. For permission to use material from this book please contact the publisher.

Published by Poems for Pleasure Press LLC ,
contact@poemsforpleasurepress.com
Stoughton, Wisconsin, United States of America
Order books online at www.PoemsforPleasurePress.com

Publisher's Cataloging-In-Publication Data
(Prepared by The Donohue Group, Inc.)

Names: Glover, Jeffry (Jeffry Keith), 1946- author. | Bausman, Mary, cover designer.
Title: 9 lively cat tales and other pet poems / Jeffry Glover ; [cover by Mary Bausman].
Other Titles: Nine lively cat tales and other pet poems
Description: First edition. | Stoughton, Wisconsin : Poems for Pleasure Press, 2019.
Identifiers: ISBN 9781948854009 (hardcover) | ISBN 9781948854016 (softcover) | ISBN 9781948854030 (ebook)
Subjects: LCSH: Cats--Poetry. | Pets--Poetry. | BISAC: POETRY / American General. | HUMOR / Topic / Animals. | PETS / Cats / General. | LCGFT: Poetry. | Stories in rhyme.
Classification: LCC PS3607.L6844 A619 2019 (print) | LCC PS3607.L6844 (ebook) | DDC 811/.6--dc23

Library of Congress Control Number:2019910737

Cover design and illustration by Mary Bausman. Editing Assistance by KJ Forest. Interior book design by Adept Content Solutions LLC with initial book layout © 2017 BookDesignTemplates.com under multi-book license. Font software: © 2010 Sebastian Kosch (sebastian@aldusleaf.org) with reserved font name "Crimson Text" and © 2016 The Nunito Project Authors (contact@sansoxygen.com) with reserved font name "Nunito Sans" licensed under the SIL Open Font License, Version 1.1 available at https://scripts.sil.org/OFL. Author photo by Express Portraits.

To support sustainability Poems for Pleasure Press books are printed by Ingram on responsibly sourced, acid-free, archival quality paper meeting the American National Standard for Informational Sciences – Permanence of Paper for Printed Library Materials, per www.ingramspark.com/environmental-responsibility.

First Edition 2019
Printed in the Unites States of America

Contents

Introductory Poems 1
   A Cat, My Muse 3
   So Many Pet Poems 3
I. 9 Lively Cat Tales 5
   Cat Bath 7
   Tale of the Perspicacious Cat 8
   Tale from Katmandu 10
   Goldfish Dreams 14
   Tyger, Tyger 17
   A Cat Went Fishing 18
   Tiger Tale 20
   The Last Bast Lesson Ever 23
   Who Will Bell the Cat? 25
II. Cuddly Kitty Characters 29
   Little Tyger 31
   Maxie 32
   Maxie Rules 33
   Maxie on Our Bed 36
   What Mew? 38
   Come, Kitty, Kitty 39
   Cats and Sleep 40
   To Categorize Two Cats 41
   Smitten by Kitten 42
III. Tales with Catitude 43
   Catitude 45
   Caturday 46

  A Most Impertinent Kitty Cat. 25
  A Cat's Demand 50
  Feral Cats. 51
  What's With Our Cat?. 52
  Your Lucky House Cat 53
  Cat at Work. 54
  The Cat Game. 55
IV. Cat and Mouse Adventures. 57
  Pussy-cat, Pussy-cat 59
  Cat Gift 60
  A Crouching Cat. 61
  The Cat from Nice 62
  What Kind of Cat?. 64
  In Praise of Alley Cats 66
  Rats for Cats, Not Bats. 67
  Cat Spat 68
  Magnifi-cat 69
V. Cat Fancies. 71
  A Leopard In a Leotard 73
  Morris, the Math Cat. 76
  If Lear Were Here. 77
  Pedicure Recompense 78
  The Lynx. 80
  A Lazy Lion. 81
  Why the Lynx Isn't Famous 82
  Notice from the Lion 84
  The Manx 85
VI. Feline Troubles. 87
  An Incorrigible Cat. 89
  The Neighborhood Cat Lady. 92
  Yowly Alley Cats. 94
  Herding Wild Cats 95
  Cat Lesson 96
  Saving a Lady's Cat. 98
  Cat Wouldn't Fiddle. 101

  Cats of Ancient Egypt 102
  Harbor Cat. 103
VII. Wild Cat Tales 105
  The Cheetah 107
  The Cougar 108
  The Leopard 109
  Save the Tyger. 111
  The Ocelot. 112
  The Jaguar 113
  Afri-cats 114
  The Polecat and Panther 115
  The Liger 116
VIII. Bow-wow, Meow, and Moo 117
  Bow-wow, Meow, and Moo 119
  A Parakeet and a Cat 122
  The Two-tailed Tomcat. 124
  Chary Birds 125
  Not Real News 126
  Hark, the Bark! 127
  Thin Dog, Fat Cat. 128
  Better Dog Days Done 129
  Tale of Caution 130
IX. Doggie Tales 131
  A Dog's Concerns 133
  A Puppy's Way 134
  My Wiener Dog 135
  Puppy Fears 136
  My Dog, Ben 137
  What Dogs Do 138
  Red 139
  No Good Goodbye 140
  Walk the Dog 142
About the Author 145

Preface

As one who has always appreciated the charming nature of cats and dogs in my life, it gives me great pleasure to present this collection of amusing tales in verse for your enjoyment. *9 Lively Cat Tales and Other Pet Poems* brings you and your fellow felinophiles and ailurophiles nine sets of rhyming poems with nine poems each, which seems appropriate since tradition tells us that cats have nine lives. In these pages you will find felines of all kinds, from pet cats to wild cats both real and fanciful, along with a few beloved dogs. You'll meet a cat who needs encouragement to take a bath, a clever math-whiz cat, a pet cat named Maxie who rules the house, a sleepy cat dreaming of catching goldfish, a fashion-conscious leopard on a shopping trip, a catena of cats with catitude, tigers, jaguars, a lynx, and an ocelot more. I hope you'll have fun reading these poems and sharing them with your family and friends. Visit *www.jeffryglover.com* to preview and order my books. Thank you.

J.G.

Acknowledgements

I wish to gratefully acknowledge and thank those who have assisted me in producing this book at Poems for Pleasure Press LLC, first and foremost KJ Forest, managing editor, for her encouragement, advice, editing, and unstinting technical assistance; my wonderful cover illustrator, Mary Bausman; Lori Martinsek and the book production team at Adept Content Solutions; my marvelous readers, and all those who have offered support and assistance along the way.

While writing this book I have drawn inspiration from many sources, including the poems "Ode on the Death of a Favourite Cat Drowned in a Tub of Goldfishes" by Thomas Gray, "The Tiger" by William Blake, the classic nursery rhyme "Pussy-cat, Pussy-cat," the recounting of "The Least Successful Animal Rescue," by Robert Fulghum in *Words I Wish I Wrote* (Cliff Street Books: New York, 1997), and the rhyme "The Owl and the Pussy-Cat" by Edward Lear.

Introductory Poems

A Cat, My Muse

My muse, a cat, inspires me
With mews to use in poetry
That when purr-used is sure to be
The cat's pajamas and bee's knees,
Not that I claim this kitty collection
Achieves the ultimate purr-fection,
But happily I think you'll see
It's fun to read, a treasury
You can encourage friends and others
 (Mothers, fathers, sisters, brothers)
To sample also with attention,
And if I may make this suggestion
To give your friends a laugh and lift,
Share this book -- make it a gift!

So Many Pet Poems

The poems I've written in my day
Are long and short ones, most for play,
Plain ones, fancy, and a few
Sillier than a curlicue.
But what could I do with so many written
About cats and dogs and a lively kitten?
Publish them in a book brand new,
Especially for amusing you.

I.
9 Lively Cat Tales

Cat Bath

Ever give your cat a bath?
My, cats love it so!
We gave our kitty one today,
So you see we know.

Got him wrestled in the tub,
Washed him in warm water,
Made him feel so clean and good
As any kitty oughter.

Soaped him up without a scratch,
Just four hands required;
Held him firmly, rinsed him off,
Just what he desired.

Finally done, we toweled him down.
He helped by shaking, too.
So go and bathe your cat today;
He'll love it, we promise you!

Tale of the Perspicacious Cat

In the city of Cass
Lived a smart kitty cat,
Who was brilliant, in fact,
Mighty sharp with his math.

Adding figures and such
He liked very much,
And subtracting them, oooh,
Was a pleasure to do.

He could calculate pi,
Count the stars in the sky,
And trees in a wood;
Indeed understood

Calculus, too,
Which he liked to pursue,
And never grew weary
Of using set theory.

This cat grew ecstatic
Solving problems quadratic
And never would lack for
Equations to factor.

He did long division
When need had arisen,
Was great with statistics
And log characteristics.

Oh, his spirits were buoyant
When he moved a decimal poyant,
While he saw in his fractions
Delightful attractions.

Yes, a polymath, he
With a fine Ph.D.,
When a square root was found,
He would purr up and down.

Such a smart kitty cat
From the city of Cass
Had a high brain capacity
And great perspicacity.

What else need we say?
He's still famous today.
Such genius is rare
As we're all well aware.

Tale from Katmandu

In the sky-high Himalayas,
Land of Everest and K2,
In a valley of Nepal
Sits the city, Katmandu.

To the north great mountains stand
Reaching to the thin-air sky;
To the south lay fearful forests
Where forbidding monsters lie.

Lurking tigers stalk and wander,
Elephants and leopards, too,
Rhinos, wolves, and vipers there,
Stuff of legends, but who knew?

"Don't go near that dreadful forest,"
A mother cautioned her young son.
"Stay close to home and gather kindling,
Chores must come before your fun."

Dutifully, the boy went walking,
Searching for the firewood,
Careless of his mother's warning,
Hardly heard or understood.

Past the outskirts of the village
He went looking here and there,
Finding sticks with little thought
Of any dangers to beware.

By and by a bamboo forest
Came in view; he ventured in.
Its shadowed darkness did not scare him
Where his real work would begin.

Past the edge he walked in deeper.
Trees and vines crisscrossed the sky,
Where he gathered brittle bamboo,
Canes he found to stack and tie.

Soon he'd gathered up a bundle
He could carry on his back
Held together with a jute rope
Fastened to his haversack.

Just a few more canes he wanted;
Then he'd have to hurry home.
Soon he had them, more than plenty;
This son was no lazybones.

As he turned to go, beginning,
Just ahead, what caught his eye?
Something spotted, something springing
From a tree--a cat up high!

Down it plunged--by luck it missed him.
Frightened, he let out a cry,
Grabbed the bundle from his back,
Knowing it was do or die,

Shoved the bundle at the leopard,
Whack! It smacked its fearsome face
Stunning it for just a moment;
Then he ran as cat gave chase.

Through the bamboo running, dashing,
Through the jungle he must pass
Ran the boy with leopard closing,
Plunging through the bamboo grass.

Suddenly the boy remembered
As he scampered for his life
Something that might help to save him:
On his belt he had a knife.

All seemed lost by now or nearly.
One chance left, he wheeled about,
Faced the cat, his knife unsheathing,
Jabbing at the leopard's snout.

With a scream the cat retreated,
Deeply cut, its fervor gone.
Luck and pluck and desperation
Had defeated feline brawn.

Poor boy, he stood panting, shaking,
Numb from what had just transpired.
Death had passed him by, but barely.
Suddenly he felt dead tired.

Knife all bloody, held before him,
Bamboo scattered, disarrayed.
For his carelessness he knew now
With his life he'd nearly paid.

Night was coming; home he hastened
With his knife and bamboo, too.
Wiser now, the boy was chastened;
One great lesson now he knew.

Home at last, his mother waiting,
"Son, why were you out so long?
You have given me a worry,
Wondering where you had gone."

"Never fear, here's bamboo plenty,
I have gathered for our fire,"
Said the boy, "A bundle heavy,
Quite enough to make me tire."

"Sit down, son, and rest yourself.
Dinner will be ready soon,"
Said his mother. "I've been baking
Ever since this afternoon."

Down he sat, but felt so sleepy,
Dinner came and dinner went.
Through it all he slept and deeply,
Mother seeing he was spent.

When he woke, she fed him plenty,
Filled him up with rice and stew.
He deserved it, he had earned it
There in Nepal, Katmandu.

Goldfish Dreams *

A kitty slept, if not content,
Yet dozing as cats do,
Relaxed at least, her paws half-bent;
She dreamed a dream came true.

Her dream entailed a gleaming fish,
A goldfish in her view.
To feast on it was her fond wish,
Better if there be two,

Two fine fish in a clear glass bowl;
My, but they looked good
To catch and bone, or gobble whole,
To savor if she could,

Except these fish were kept up high,
So high this cat must leap,
When far away from owner's eye
To reach them thence to eat.

Indeed, the cat must nearly fly,
An effort great to make,
Provided that she dared to try,
If she were wide awake,

Safer, though, to sleep and dream
Of reaching this fishbowl,
In slumber a delightful scheme
For catching fish, her goal.

She twitched her tail and perked her ears;
To catch them was her plan,
Her fantasy and absent fears,
To forego fish from can,

Though cans can yield what fresh may not,
Far safer than live fish.
No cat should carp when what they've got
Is salmon in their dish.

Still the kitty dreamed she'd try
In her imagination.
The bowl she judged was not *that* high,
Just needed concentration.

The jump she thought was fifteen feet,
Her prospects rather stark.
She'd need a catapult to leap
And hit that high a mark.

Atop her sofa there she stood
Deciding what to do,
Calculating if she could
Procure a fish (or two),

Where both were swimming unaware
Around their bowl with ease,
Oblivious to kitty there,
Or fishies she might seize.

Finally, the moment came:
By mighty spring and leap,
A chance for great success and fame
To feast or fail and weep!

Was it a dream, or was it real,
Did cat catch fish or not?
What happened next? We do not know
Whether fish were caught.

We cannot say that fish serene
Were savored as cat's prey,
Or swam more nights in kitty's dream,
Not made into fillet.

Apologies we offer you;
Fish for answers as we may.
Cat's got our tongues. What can we do?
Did kitty leap that day?

We cannot this reveal to you,
Although it is our wish.
Go query cat for her meow
Or try and ask the fish!

---

*See also "Ode on the Death of a Favourite Cat, Drowned in a Tub of Goldfishes" by the 18th century poet Thomas Gray.

Tyger, Tyger *

Tyger, tyger, what a fright
To encounter one at night,
Worse perhaps if it were day
And you couldn't run away.

Oh, what trembling, oh what fear,
If you knew that one were near,
If it saw you had no chance
Without a gun or even lance,

Sensed your chances to survive
Were slim to none to stay alive,
That you'd be done-for, caught by paws
And torn to pieces in its jaws,

If it found you, like a deer,
In the open, in the clear,
Didn't see it, couldn't hear
Until the tyger would appear.

Tyger, tyger, what a sight,
Cat of a very savage stripe,
Not the kind with which to play,
Better, then, to stay away.

Paw note:

Felines living behind bars
In our zoos the biggest stars,
Tygers, tygers, do you grieve,
Burning, wishing you could leave?

---
* With apologies to William Blake.

A Cat Went Fishing

There was a cat went fishing,
A fishing cat was he,
And found a catfish swishing
Its tail quite casually.

"I have a tale to tell,"
The fish said to the cat.
"If you will just sit still."
Said cat, "I can do that."

Cat put his pole aside,
He put his hook away,
He perked up both his ears
To hear fish have his say.

"My story starts like this,"
The catfish soon began,
"When I was just a minnow,
Much faster then I swam,

"Because much bigger fish,
Far larger ones than I
Would snap at me and wish
To eat me, that is why

"I had to swim so fast;
I had to dart and hide
If I was going to last,
In short, just stay alive.

"It wasn't always easy
To swim and not be slow.
Before a carp could seize me,
I really had to go!

"But I was quick and clever;
I often swam at night
And hid in weeds wherever
I wasn't in plain sight.

"A year passed first, then two,
And now just look at me.
I grew and grew and grew
Until eventually

"I am as I am here,
No longer short or small.
I'm braver with less fear,
And larger overall.

"Yes, sir, now I am wise.
I know about fish hooks.
I'm harder to surprise.
I've read more storybooks.

"And so I say, sir cat,
Go home and mew, tisk-tisk.
You cannot catch me at
My age, not this catfish!"

Therefore the cat went home
To eat a tuna salad,
Accepting what he'd heard,
Believing it was valid,

And told this story to
His children, all his kits,
And claimed it must be true,
How the catfish used its wits.

Tiger Tale

"Yo' tiger, there, you, out of sight,
Hidden in yon dappled light,
My, you've given me a fright,
Not to say you'd ever bite.

"Still, tiger, I don't know you well
As friend or foe; I just can't tell,
And since you wear no warning bell,
Trusting you is a hard, hard sell.

"I'd like to trust you, understand,
Not just reject you out of hand,
But I don't know what you have planned
Lying there in jungle land."

"Trust, indeed!" the tiger said.
"If you're a tourist, I'll bet you've read
Those silly, lying, gory stories
About us tigers. Well, I'm sorry.

"It's most unfair to believe such tales,
So untrue in their details.
What falsehoods and fables these days one meets,
And rumors about what a tiger eats,

"Like humans, for instance, a bunch of baloney,
Exaggerations! Lies! Fake news only.
I'd never do such things as that.
Don't you know—*I'm just a cat!*

"It's a simple fact, cats love to purr.
We're soft as silk—come feel my fur.
Loved and pampered, we'd never eat
One of you for our lunch meat.

"Our menus feature the mad March Hare
Found around here and most everywhere
And birds we snatch out of the air.
There are too many, so who's to care?

"We prefer to keep our bellies svelte,
Play whatever paw we're dealt,
And respect the law. We've always felt
When times are tough, we should tighten our belt."

"Hmm, put that way, you might be right,"
Says I to tiger. "Why be up-tight?
You are, after all, lying in plain sight;
Then again, maybe not, not quite.

"It's hard to see you in dappled light.
Maybe if I squint, since the light's not bright.
I mean you no harm nor any slight.
There, now you're in my line of sight."

Said the tiger, "Friend, just relax.
I assure you, a tiger never attacks.
I have right here reliable facts,
Which your guidebook likely lacks.

"Come take my picture, won't you, please?
Put down your guns. You won't need these.
Fear isn't good. It's like a disease.
To take the best photos, get down on your knees."

"We mustn't quarrel," the tiger sighed.
"Come closer here to where I hide
Under cover in the brush and trees
Where it's shady and cool, there's a lovely breeze."

The tiger was brilliant, now wasn't he,
To offer his hide-out and hospitality?
So how do you think things all turned out?
Can you picture it? Is there any doubt?

Need we say much more how the story ends?
What good was suspicion between true friends?
As the photographer approached down on his knees,
Gun-less, fearless, at his ease,

He felt the breeze; yes, there it was
As the tiger sprang (as every cat does.)
That son-of-a-gun tiger loaded his chops
Before the photographer could change f-stops.

Oh, what a feast--for the tiger at least,
Though hard to swallow for the deceased,
Whose days had sadly quickly passed
To the dismay of those who watched, aghast.

Not much is left to say from here
Except be careful and be sure
To pay attention to your fears,
Since all is not as first appears.

The Last Bast Lesson Ever *

In the delta of the Nile
Dwelt a hungry crocodile,
Sneaky, ancient, full of guile;
Planning breakfast made him smile.

While on the bank of the river sat
Bast, named for the goddess cat,
Worshipped daily, fair and pretty,
In Bubastis, Bast's sacred city.

All the pharaohs pampered her,
Fed her well and stroked her fur.
Like protective daughter of sun god, Ra,
She was praised and held in awe

Until one morning, through the fog,
She observed a floating log
Gliding in her general direction;
That, at least, was her first impression.

Approaching slowly came the log,
Low, half hidden by the fog,
Till it reached the very place
Where Bast sat in regal grace,

Careless, dreaming, half awake.
She was dozing – big mistake!
When a crocodile named Sobek,
From the Nile suddenly leapt!

In a flash its mighty jaws
Grasped poor Bast; its vicious claws
Dragged her helpless into the river.
(Poor kitty cat; it makes one shiver!)

So ended an incautious cat of Bubastis
Snatched by the fiercest and the fastest
Crock who dared attack Bast's cult,
Adding death to cruel insult.

If you should think this tale's a crock,
Think again, for it is not.
Never let your first impression
Lead you to an indiscretion,

Or catch you in a mighty mess,
More than you would ever guess,
Even lead to your demise;
Stay alert, on guard; be wise.

---

* Note: Bast, ancient Egyptian goddess of joy, music, and dancing, was personified as a cat who protected Ra, the sun god, from attack. Bubastis, located in the Nile delta, was a city at the center of Bast's cult. Sobek was the ancient Egyptian crocodile god, whose relationship with other gods was complicated!

Who Will Bell the Cat?

"Who will bell our cat today?"
A rat asked of his kind.
A bell could keep the cat at bay
When loose, and not confined,

"But left outside its home alone
It roams and hunts for us.
We need to hear when it is near;
A bell would be a plus.

"We want a volunteer, someone
Who's brave and quick and clever,
A rat that's strong and likes to run
Who'll take on this endeavor."

"I'll do the deed," said one brash rat.
"I'll bell that mean old cat.
But who has got the bell I'll need?
Let me ask you that."

"I have one hanging in my cage,"
Chirped a canary bird.
"When I want my birdseed wage,
I peck it to be heard."

This tinkle bell was promptly fetched;
The rat's request was met,
With bell to bell the cat, that wretch,
The best bell they could get.

But when the brash rat saw the bell,
Well, what do you suppose?
He got a chill, did not feel well,
With fear he nearly froze.

It seems he'd had a second thought.
With all the task entailed.
He worried, what if he were caught?
Alas, his courage failed.

To volunteer was one thing, but
Far harder to do the deed.
He said to his comrades, "Tell you what,
I'm not so good at speed,

"Which is required to risk my neck
And do this daring deed,
And to succeed as you expect
I'd need greased-lightning speed.

"Were I to grow here big and strong
To a super rat degree,
Then maybe I'd try bell the cat
And make rat history.

"But fear has found my rodent heart
And will not let me try.
I value my life way too much
And do not wish to die.

"Please pardon me. I hope you see
That even if I could
Bell the cat, my family
Would insist I never should.

"Too dangerous the task would be
And prone to tragedy.
I'm quite averse I've come to see
To risks of this degree.

"And so I beg your pardon here.
Alas, I must recant
The pledge I made and make it clear
To bell the cat I shan't."

The rats were cross as you might guess
To hear his humble speech,
And have him fearfully confess
Their goal beyond his reach.

The cat, of course, did not suspect.
He'd not have cared one whit
If a rat tried bell his neck
And so that's how things sit,

Or should we say how they have sat
Between the rats and cat,
And will stay to their dismay,
Alas, that's a matter of fact.

The lesson here: don't volunteer
Unless you're truly brave,
Don't break a promise out of fear
And dignity you'll save.

Though if bravery is your thing,
Follow it to the end.
Find a bell and make it ring,
You might succeed, my friend.

II.
Cuddly Kitty Characters

Little Tyger

Tyger, tyger, well, not quite,
Kitten on my lap tonight,
Oh, what purring, my, my, my,
You are doing, wonder why.

You're like a little motorboat
Some would think to hear your throat.
William Blake, were he right here,
Would approve, I'm pretty sure.

Little tyger, my delight,
Would you like some milk tonight,
Or perhaps a can of fish,
Something good to fill your dish?

As for symmetry and such,
You needn't worry very much.
Were you larger, that might be
Of some concern eventually.

Being small now, all is well;
You're not so fierce, truth to tell.
Fear not, for we'll keep petting thee
While you purr on contentedly.

Maxie

We have a cat—his name is Maxie.
He may look fierce, but he's not attackie.
In fact, he's refined as a cat can be,
Smartly groomed and gentlemanly.

We serve him three meals every day,
As he demands—that's his way.
Should we delay, he'll complain, and how!
Loudly with a firm "Meow!"

With no claws he's no match
For our sofa, he cannot scratch.
When we open a door, Maxie has tried
To sneak past us to venture outside.

But defenseless without claws and cars whizzing past
We keep him inside so his nine lives last.
When neighborhood cats come to our door,
Maxie acts bored. He wonders what for.

At night he prefers to sleep on our bed
Down round our feet or curled up near my head.
During daytime he's casual, often pauses to yawn,
But should a stranger stop by—whoosh!—he is gone!

Like most other cats, we definitely find
Maxie is certainly of independent mind,
Not a bad way to be for a cat
Since wherever he is, he knows where he's at.

That's the life of our Maxie, pretty soft it would seem,
Well-fed, warm bed, a kitty cat's dream.
He's a prince of a pet living life like a king.
Ask him what else he needs, he will purr, "Not a thing."

Maxie Rules

As we have mentioned heretofore,
We have a cat whom we adore;
He's quiet, tame, and a little wacky
And rules our roost quite matter-of-factly.

At mealtimes he is more than clear
Meowing, "Give me chow, you hear?"
In fact, when dining, night and day
He expects to have his way.

At dinner, if he wants light tuna
He demands it quick or even soonah,
Preferring it served in a silver dish,
Fresh as tomorrow he wants his fish.

Though it's quite beneath him ever to beg,
He's known to hint; he'll rub our leg
To tell us what is on his mind,
That's how he reminds us it's feeding time.

His rule is this: "I am the cat;
I'll let you share my habitat,
But don't presume I'll let you stay
Unless, of course, you me obey."

So Maxie lives like royalty
Pampered, room and board both free.
Indeed, he considers our house his castle
Where we must serve him without hassle.

And when the light begins to fall
And fade against our bedroom wall,
Maxie saunters, jumps, and goes
Up on our bed and licks his toes.

One might suppose this little trait
Of licking his toes may just equate
To a warm sponge-bath which you or I
Might choose to take, but we ask why,

Why would a cat clean all four paws
Or sharply polish up his claws?
What, we ask, might this habit mean?
Yuck! Think of where his paws have been!

Perhaps he's pawed some dry dust bunny
Crawling under our bed on his tummy,
Or swatted a spider, a moth or bug,
Then licked his paws--think of it. Ugh!

Yet Maxie acts like he's so refined,
An elegant gentleman and much inclined
To show he's svelte, smooth, soft to touch,
Requiring petting and preening much.

When I'm away, I never know
Where Maxie slinks or deigns to go:
On my table for inspection
Or curled up on a chair for introspection.

Perhaps he sleeps, or chases around.
We've seen him run and even bound.
Or he might pounce on a cotton string.
Who knows? He might do anything,

Like party with a hapless mouse,
Not likely though, not in our house.
Perhaps he chases his fluffy tail,
Catches and bites it, and makes a wail.

Most likely, we think he sleeps a lot
On my reading chair, his favorite spot.
He's happy there; from this throne he rules
And does not suffer any fools.

We tell you this just so you know,
If to our house you should go,
You'll know the rules as a matter of fact,
Exactly how Maxie expects you to act.

You'll know without question who's in charge;
Not humans like us, by and large,
But rather, him with four paws for feet.
He'll look you over, so be discreet.

Take our advice; it's for the best:
Follow Maxie's rules if you're our guest.
Do this with care, act with tact,
And you'll pass inspection when you meet our cat.

Maxie on Our Bed

As we have noted, it's a matter of fact
That we have a regal family cat,
One we adore, and though well-bred,
He prefers to sleep on our featherbed.

We'd really prefer, because Maxie sheds,
That he go and sleep somewhere else instead.
But on this issue, sleeping on our bed,
Maxie is stubborn; we're at loggerheads.

Besides, every morning, this must be said,
He insists, nay, requires his breakfast in bed,
Plus he wakes up early from the living dead
Demanding his due, that kitty punkinhead.

And if we put him out, he paws at the door,
Which does not amuse at a quarter to four.
He keeps on meowing, till we hear what he's said,
A nightly performance that we've come to dread.

If we let him back in, he will jump on the bed
And be entertained by our pulling a thread.
Then he'll preen himself for an hour or so
Like he's a king on his throne running the show.

We fear there's no cure, none we can find,
That would change our cat or make him mind.
Should we accept what we cannot ignore,
Plug our ears and lock the door?

Maxie, please know, we must have our sleep.
Need to have shut-eye, comfy and deep,
Undisturbed zzz's to rest a poor head,
For slumber that's peaceful when we go to bed.

It isn't we don't love you, cat, truly we do,
It's just that ... just that ... we need sleep, and you ...
Oh, all right, you little stinker, forget what we said,
Come on back in and sleep on the bed!

What Mew?

Say, kitty, kitty, what sound do I hear?
Do I detect a mew?
Have you a problem or a fear,
Is there something bothering you?

Are you fearing we are out of fish
To feed your growling tummy?
Or have you some fine feline wish
For food that's much more yummy?

Did sparrows you had hoped to catch
Escape your stealthy paws,
Or unawares, a nuthatch perhaps
Eluded your claws and jaws?

Cry "Fowl!" kitty. Life's unfair.
We sympathize, poor dear,
But other days, please be aware,
May bring you prey to cheer!

For now amuse yourself with hope
And maybe something nice
Will come along to help you cope,
If not a bird, think mice!

Come, Kitty, Kitty

Come, kitty, kitty, out from under the bed;
Poor dear, no need to hide your head.
The dog that scared you has gone away;
It's no wonder that you fled.

Come, kitty, kitty, it's safe to play.
We've sent that wag-tag dog away.
No need to fear; he's not here now;
You're safe, it's all okay.

Come, kitty, kitty, oh what a sight
To see you tremble from such a fright.
We heard you hiss, then hide like this.
Now everything's all right.

No need to shiver hiding here.
The dog's long gone, so have no fear.
It's safe to come out, safe for sure;
The dog won't reappear.

Look what we've brought you--see, a treat,
Sardines! Your favorite food to eat,
And a saucer of milk to coax you out
To calm your nerves, my sweet.

Come, kitty, kitty, that's the way.
Here's a string, come out and play.
Chase it with your pretty paws.
Come out now, what do you say?

Come, kitty, kitty, I'll pet your fur
The way you like, how you prefer.
Everything's all better now.
Come out, let's hear you purr.

Cats and Sleep

Cat's rarely find they cannot sleep,
And never need to count their sheep.
When they want to catch a wink
They close their eyes and never think:
Am I tired? Should I rest?
Will I find I'll be my best
If I fail to take a nap
Curled up on a comfy lap?
Thoughts like this do not apply.
Cats just pause and down they lie.
Which is what most cats prefer,
As can be told by how they purr.
Doing this is what they choose,
When and where they wish to snooze.

To Categorize Two Cats

Two cats have we, one young, one old,
A timid cat, the other bold.
Why this is so, we do not know,
But one moves fast, the other slow.
"Stop" and "Go" are their names,
"Catch Mouse," or "String," their favorite games.
Domestic cats they are for sure,
Content to snooze and be demure,
Although at times with eyes all wide
They watch small birds flit by outside.
But be assured beyond a doubt
We never let them, either, out.
Yet on the whole they both aver
By purr, inside they much prefer.

Smitten by Kitten

When my daughter turned four, we promised her that
We'd go to a pet store and find her a cat.
So off we went. It wasn't far,
Driving together in our family car.

As we entered the store, she cried, "Follow me!"
And scampered off to find her kitty.
In a corner of the place way toward the back,
We found two kittens, one white, one black.

Of the two, one was small,
Looking like a snowball,
Fun to hold, soft to touch,
We all liked her very much.

"Let's take her home," daughter said to me.
"This one? All right." We had to agree.
So we held her close, took her home from the store.
Well, today my daughter is ten, not four.

Snowball has become our cat, from a kitten,
Since that first day when we were smitten.

III.
Tales with Catitude

Catitude

What word is it that best describes
The nature of a cat?
We've pondered this and theorized,
And based on how they act

It's "catitude," like attitude,
Though these aren't quite the same.
The first is more specific
To a feline mostly tame.

This word describes an actual cat
With independent mien,
Its manner sometimes lacking tact
Within its home domain.

Cats keep their independence,
Though close, they can seem far.
In this they really have no choice,
It's simply how cats are.

They let you pet them now and then
Depending on their mood,
But often they ignore you when
They feel that you intrude.

So "catitude," a word we lacked,
Can now be used and matched
To how cats act in point of fact,
Reserved, aloof, detached.

Caturday

Ask any feline, and they'll say,
"Every day is Caturday,"
Purrfectly and assuredly,
With confidence and certainty.
At least it's true in their view
As they'll make clear and often do.
They say, "We must be catered to
Where and when we make our mew,
'Cause cats come first without exception
Epitomizing cat purrfection,
Soft and subtle as we are,
The best of animals by far,
Wonderful in every way,
So every day is Caturday."

A Most Impertinent Kitty Cat

One day I found a kitty cat
On my doorstep where it sat.
It said, "You're in my habitat."
And I replied, "Be gone, cat. Scat!"

He didn't blink, but rambled in
Between my legs, for he was thin
And black. His meowing made a din.
He claimed to be my long-lost kin.

I retorted, "No you're not!"
Didn't faze him. He asked what
Food I had on the spot,
And I replied, "Not a lot."

"Mister," he said, "how about tonight
You grill some fish the way I like?
For tuna is my great delight.
It satisfies my appetite."

So what was I supposed to do?
The cat was in my house. I knew
To throw him out, although I might,
Would just seem mean and impolite.

So I grilled his tuna steak,
And watched him hungrily partake.
He dashed it down, for goodness sake,
Then slept as if he'd never wake.

When he awoke, he ordered me
To serve him up a cup of tea,
"Poured," he said, quite pleasantly,
"To serve me reverentially."

So I served him tea steeped hot
With cookies that would hit the spot.
But did he thank me? You know what?
Not one word of thanks I got.

After tea, what did he do?
Asked for cash to see him through!
Said he had business to pursue,
That needed cash and hurry, too.

I said, "Cat, you ask a lot."
He cried, "Ten bucks? That's all you've got?
I've bills to pay for stuff I've bought."
I said, "Look cat, it's rich I'm not.

"Listen here, I'm nearly broke.
You'll drain me dry, and that's no joke.
If I had an egg, you'd want the yoke."
The kitty mewed, "You're a misanthrope!"

"No," I said, "but my generosity
Has got to stop--you're soaking me.
Dog gone it, I'm no money tree.
Now go away and leave me be."

The kitty yowled, "Have it your way!
I've got better things to do today.
If you're this stingy, if you won't pay,
I'll take my leave and find other prey."

At that the greedy kitty cat
I showed the door and shouted "Scat!"
This time he left my habitat,
Sauntered away, and that was that.

So ends the tale (knock on wood!)
Of how a cat would, if it could,
Move in on you. Understood?
Then heed this warning and you'll be good.

A Cat's Demand

A cat is a creature you will find
Of more than independent mind.
It tells you when it wants its fill
Of fish, insists you foot the bill,
Or it will mew so loud and steady,
At last you'll say, "Alright already,"
And give in to its strong demand
Just as your kitty cat has planned.

Feral Cats

Wild cats often here appear,
Feral cats who have no fear,
Savvy felines from the street
Who smell food and want to eat.
On holidays or any time
Regardless, they will come to dine
Scrounging for small scraps of dinner
In our trash cans (they have been here)
Thinner than our cats at home,
More independent, left alone,
Kings of the road or queens, whichever,
Survivors, really, rather clever,
And so we see them now and then,
Yet never knowing where or when.

What's With Our Cat?

What is it with our cat? I swear
He's haughty, naughty, hard to bear,
Puts on airs like he's king of this place,
Says to address him as "Your Catship" or "Grace,"
And should we, heaven forbid, forget
To feed him on time, he has a hissy fit
Claiming we are here to serve
Him every mouse, morsel, or hors d'oeuvre
He requests, demands … and get this:
Woe to us if we resist!
Because, you see, he claims he's royal
And we, his subjects, to be loyal
Must cat-er to his every wish
By which he means to feed him fish!

Your Lucky House Cat

For many a lucky cat
A house is their habitat,
A place to eat and sleep
With room and board dirt cheap.

They really have it made
Since meals and rent are paid,
And most are well aware
Life's cushy living there.

There's string to chase and such,
They like this very much
To keep them on their toes
With pleasure, and it shows.

Then when they want their chow,
They've merely to meow,
Meander to their dish
And feast on tuna fish.

So that's where things are at
For your typical pampered cat.

Cat at Work

She walks like sleep
Quiet sneaks
Toward the bird
Yet unheard
Then she leaps
And no more cheeps

The Cat Game

It was a game we played:
Our cat would make a dash
Out the front door, unafraid,
She'd sneak to reach the grass.
If we didn't catch her quick,
Grab her and go in,
She'd eat green grass, get sick
As if that was "her win"!
We never let her reach the street,
She wouldn't get that far,
Though she'd scamper, even leap.
She'd try ... that's how cats are.
And all her life she never knew
What dangers lurked when cars sped through.

IV.
Cat and Mouse Adventures

Pussy-cat, Pussy-cat

Pussy-cat, pussy-cat, where have you been?
I've been to London to look at the queen.
Pussy-cat, pussy-cat, what did you there?
I frightened a little mouse under her chair.

—Classic Nursery Rhyme

Pussy-cat, pussy-cat, what said the queen?
She shrieked, "Catch that mouse!" And she made quite a scene.
Pussy-cat, pussy-cat, what did the mouse?
Laughed, for he knew he had brought down the house.
Pussy-cat, pussy-cat, do you mean castle?
Yes, where the mouse lived, that quick little rascal.
Pussy-cat, pussy-cat, was the mouse sought?
Yes, and I'm proud to say, by me was caught.
Pussy-cat, pussy-cat, did you feel sorry?
No, since the queen saw I got all the glory.
Pussy-cat, pussy-cat, what kind of glory?
Honors galore and she made me a marquis.
Pussy-cat, pussy-cat, what else can you tell me?
My belly is full--that's the end of my story.

Cat Gift

A scaredy-cat lives at our house;
She rarely goes outside
And wouldn't catch a vole or mouse;
To see one, she'd just hide,

Or so we thought until the day
A wandering mouse got in.
Our shy cat caught it right away
And proud, presented him.

To her good credit and our surprise,
She dropped it at our feet.
A gift it was, her precious prize,
She would not think to eat.

From this our cat has gained respect,
A rise in estimation,
Now known as "mouser," not just pet
With rebuilt reputation!

A Crouching Cat

A cat is crouching close to cheese
When a hungry mouse he sees
To seize if he is fast and clever,
Which depends a lot on whether

The cat has patience, also skill,
To catch the mouse he wants to kill.
It may seem savage of the cat,
But this is how things work, and that

Is how the contest usually goes,
As you and I and most suppose
If the cat is on his toes,
Especially those experienced pros.

The encounter will be short and sweet
(Cat's point of view) who wants to eat,
But if the cat is new at this,
His first try may just go amiss,

Which could become for cat a lesson,
Though in the long-run a real blessin'
Leading to, well, more or less,
With practice, later, much success.

The Cat from Nice

There was a cat in France from Nice,
Who lived on mice and scraps of cheese;
And every day he used to feast
On helpless mice, the cad, the beast!

The mice, of course, called this unfair.
The cat, however, did not care.
He found his mice near everywhere
And ate them singly or by the pair,

Which did not sit well with the mice,
Who seemed to feel they had no choice
But put up with this cat until
Each day it had its mousy fill.

For weeks the mice thought, thought a lot,
And tried to come up with a plot
To chase this predator away,
No longer let it prey each day.

But what, they wondered, could they do?
No mouse was sure, no mouse there knew.
The cat was big, the mice were small.
That's how it was, and that was all.

Perhaps a dog could help them, though,
A great big dog, a bowwow, so
At last they went to look for one
Who liked to chase cats just for fun.

They searched around until they found
A canine at the local pound,
A puppy who might chase a cat
Out of Nice where they were at.

One night they sneaked the puppy out.
He was the one, they had no doubt,
Who'd do what they themselves could not:
Carry out their feline plot.

First things first; they took him home,
Fed him well and let him roam
Around their neighborhood until
At last he saw the cat -- oh, thrill!

The cat was frightened, felt dismay.
The puppy chased it, wondrous play
As cat went clawing up a tree
Scared half to death immediately.

Waiting till the cat came down
Was a strategy the dog judged sound
For even cats, by and by,
Must get hungry, which is why

Waiting was the thing to do
For the pup. Mice thought so, too.
Finally, they might feel safe
With the cat put in its place.

One less cat was one less worry
And they'd be free to eat and scurry
In the city, there in Nice,
Just as much as they might please.

There you have a shaggy dog story
Of how the mice and pup won glory,
And why when cats in Nice you see
They're more than likely up a tree.

What Kind of Cat?

What kind of cat is there that
Could be afraid of moles?
A nervous cat, a scaredy-cat,
Also won't hunt voles.

She simply doesn't like such critters,
The way they run and creep,
Giving her poor heart the jitters
Disturbing her night's sleep.

Perhaps it's how our cat was raised,
An orphan we suspect,
Avoided hunting, rarely praised,
Suffered from neglect.

Confronted now by critters that
She's never seen before,
A chipmunk, rabbit, mouse or rat,
Each one she does abhor.

Running on the lawn outside
Or worse, across our floor,
From every one she'll run and hide.
She knows not what they're for.

A toy, a friend, or fearsome foe,
She really cannot tell,
She knows not what to do and so
Does nothing. Very well,

We will get another pet,
A teammate who might help,
A bona fide young puppy set
To growl and bark and yelp.

Should he find a mouse or mole,
A vole, or such as these,
The pup can play a mentor role
Easy as you please.

We got a dog to have around,
But mice they've never found.
When rodents hear our cat and hound
They hide, don't make a sound.

That's the story without glory
For this playful pair.
They've never caught a single thing
As far as we're aware.

But looking on the brighter side,
Our glass half full (with ice),
All expectations put aside,
To date we've no more mice!

In Praise of Alley Cats

It can be said of alley cats
That life is often rough.
They scrounge around, engage in spats,
And prove they're tough enough
To spend their days uncertainly,
Yet many still will thrive.
They feel no insecurity
And somehow they survive.
I've seen them feast in garbage cans;
Their tastes are far from fussy.
While rodents figure in their plans,
Of these they're fond--they must be,
And every one they catch for dinner
Makes people grateful they have been there.

Rats for Cats, Not Bats

A bat is not a flying rat,
A fact you likely know.
Wings it has that flit and flap
More rapidly than slow.
This is known by cats in theory
Who fondly chase most rats,
Which is why all rats are leery
Who encounter cats.
Indeed, we know right off the bat
That cats prefer rats' taste,
And will run fast, dash pitter-pat,
After rats they chase,
Doing so with utmost zeal
Since rats, not bats, have more appeal.

Cat Spat

Hey diddle-diddle, a cat spat up spittle
While her mother was out of the room.
A little dog gasped, grossed out by what passed,
And dashed off to fetch a spittoon.
Too late, what went on was over and done
Where upon the mom made her return,
With a look rather stern, that spoiled half the fun,
She asked her young kit, "So, did you learn
Eating green grass, though you may think it yummy,
Is not, dear, alas, all that good for your tummy?
Wherever you've been, whether outdoors or in,
Please don't do it, don't do it, ever again."
"I promise I won't, and won't trouble the puppy."
"Well, see that you don't. Spitting up is too yucky."

Magnifi-cat

To you, my kitty, I do raise,
Magnifi-cat, these words of praise,
Although I know, at least for now,
They cannot match your sweet meow,
Nor ever show in ways sublime
How much indebted to you I'm
For your softness and your touch,
Fur what it's worth, oh yes, so much,
And offer you your due applause
For steady paws and sharpened claws,
The way they move with quiet stealth
Indicative of your good health
And splendid focus of your eyes,
Especially when you're hunting mice.

V.
Cat Fancies

A Leopard in a Leotard

A leopard in a leotard
Went shopping one spring day.
He stopped for lunch, picked up two gnus,
And ate them on his way.

He entered a department store
To buy a clever hat.
"What is your business?" asked a clerk.
"I'm speaking to you, cat."

"Oh, not a thing, except I bring
My taste for fancy clothes,
Like suits and hats," declared the cat,
"And what else, heaven knows."

The clerk was puzzled--what to make
Of a leopard in his store.
He thought to serve him if he must
Or show this cat the door.

"What have you in a banker's suit?"
The leopard snarled and growled.
The clerk knew suits were then on sale
And so he simply bowed

And led the leopard to the place
Where hung his suits for sale,
Suggesting for the pants a hole
Be cut for leopard's tail.

"I'll take this one and try it on.
Now where's your changing room?"
"It's over there," the clerk replied.
"But I take my break at noon."

"I won't be long," the leopard hissed.
"Provided this suit fits,
And if it does, just ring it up.
Here clerk, a tip, two bits."

The clerk was thinking, "Kiss my grits,"
But business had been slow.
The leopard went to try the suit;
He wanted it just so.

The clerk stood by, a patient guy;
The leopard took his time.
Why hurry since he'd tipped two bits?
He could have tipped a dime.

The cat returned inside his suit,
And my, he looked so fine.
"I'll take it just the way it is,
And another here I'm buyin'.

Ring 'em up." He paid cool cash,
'Cause cash can be relied on.
The leopard left, so svelte and brash,
So suave and all in fashion.

The clerk was pleased, the leopard, too,
The best dressed cat around.
A first impression always counts
Where a cat is apt to be found.

It's only right to look one's best.
High fashion always matters,
And leaping on a wildebeest
Can tear a suit to tatters.

And so a leopard with good taste
Must often buy a new one,
One suitable to wear for work,
No matter what he's doin'.

Fancy suits are proper wear
When made to fit the bill.
It's vital that a leopard cat
Be always dressed to kill.

Morris, the Math Cat

"Irrational numbers, you see,
Extend to infinity!"
Said Morris, the cat,
One smart polymath.
"The golden ratio and pi,"
He declared, "qualify.
Such numbers, my, my,
Stretch above the blue sky,
And continue beyond
Unless rounded, go on
And on without end,"
Would Morris contend,
"Though we know not how,
They're impressive--meow!"

If Lear Were Here

If Edward Lear were ever here,
He'd tell me what to write.
If I were here with Edward Lear,
I'd listen and I might,

But since he's not, then all we've got
Are verses he once wrote,
Like "The Owl and the Pussy-cat"
In their beautiful pea green boat.

Pedicure Recompense

Once upon a time there was
A fashion-conscious kitty
Who liked to pedicure her claws
Because this made them pretty.

A pedicure was fun for her,
She got one every day,
Which gave her joy and made her purr,
But cost near all her pay.

Poor kitty cat! What could she do?
She didn't have an answer.
Her friends suggested she go to
A fortune-telling panther.

The trouble was this cost a mint
(Plus her catnip was depleted
That she'd tried to save by stint.)
She cried, "I feel defeated."

"There, there," the panther reassured
When she reached her door.
"I'll waive my fee just once, I've heard
Your story and you're poor.

"Please step inside my parlor here
And we will take a look
In my crystal ball--it's clear,"
And so they did, which took

The panther and the kitty cat
Aback by what was there,
For there they saw right off the bat
Life wasn't fair and square.

To paint cat nails near every day
Was simply too expensive.
It cost so much, there was no way
To pay fees that extensive.

She feared they'd pile up week by week
And day by day by day.
It wouldn't work, they'd have to seek
A different way to pay.

"What can we do to get me through
This quandary in a hurry?"
Asked the pretty kitty, who
Was much inclined to worry.

The panther, sorry, shook her head,
The kitty feeling faint,
And then she frowned and simply said,
"A solution, cat, there ain't

"Except you paint your own fine claws,
Don't go for pedicures.
It has to be this way because
Although desire occurs,

"The fact is, while you love high fashion,
And fashion's fun for you
When you let your pride and passion
Cause claw fees to accrue

"To bills that high, such great expense,
There is no help, nor recompense.
That's all I'll say, except go hence.
Next time my fee is twenty pence."

The Lynx

The lynx, despite what we might think,
At night hangs out at roller rinks.
By day he also likes to bowl;
His goal is better self-control.

He spares no effort for a strike,
Like an alley cat (though not his type)
Who practices his feline powers
For days on end and at all hours.

Between most games he likes to snack,
Watch others play, and stay laid back,
Exactly how he spends his time
Staying fit and in his prime.

So there we have the lynx today
Who loves to snack, skate, bowl and play.
This is his pleasure and his way
And will remain so, come what may.

A Lazy Lion

There was a lazy lion cat
Who laid around and chewed the fat,
And lived from day to day with hope
His meal would be an antelope.

There'd been a time when he was younger
He remembered feeling hunger.
In those days his life had been
Touch and go, oh so thin,

Skin and bones, to tell the truth;
That's how he'd lived in his lost youth,
Lacking any sort of pride.
Fact is, well, he nearly died.

Then one day he woke up mad.
Enough of hunger and being sad!
He noticed in the distance far, a
Safari in the Maasai Mara

And roared their way, "Hey, look at me.
Come here for your photography
And pay my fee, ten pounds of meat,
For you can see I need to eat."

The deal was made and soon he ate
Steady meals and life was great,
Never after was the same.
He'd learned the system, won the game.

Why the Lynx Isn't Famous

The lynx is not a cat with fame
Due perhaps to its strange name,
And unlike lions with shorter mane,
All reasons fame it can't obtain.

For felines like this we feel sorry,
Or should since it gets no glory.
Its size may also be to blame,
From its perspective just a shame.

So what's the lynx supposed to do?
These facts won't change because they're true.
Of course the lynx could simply lie,
But what's the use? Why even try?

The lynx could mount its own campaign,
A PR effort aimed to gain
More public notice and attention.
How about a lynx convention

Complete with national TV speeches?
After all, the media reaches
Lots of folks who might react
Well to such a dark horse cat.

Alas, this likely will not happen.
The lynx is shy, too often nappin'
In the forest undercover,
Hard to search for or discover

Where it spends its daylight time
On the ground or when it'll climb
Up a tree to take a nap,
Far too wild for a human lap,

When all it wants to do is snooze,
For humans simply has no use.
And that's the problem with the lynx,
So far its reputation stynx.

Notice from the Lion

"I'm fed up with folks calling me
'The King of Beasts' like royalty,
When "lion" is my pedigree,
Panthera leo, don't you see?
So from now on, note, I resign.
You heard me right; the thing is I'm
Not the cat to wear a crown,
The kind you hunt and then shoot down
To be a trophy in your den,
Skinned and stuffed, which has been
An awful way to rule and reign.
In fact, it's been a royal pain.
As for my Metro-Goldwyn-Mayer roar,
I will not do that anymore."

The Manx

Here's the truth about the manx,
A cat that has no tail:
When offered one, she said, "No thanks"
A remark beyond the pale,
But went on, "If I wanted tails,
I'd shop for one at Bloomingdale's.
I'd go there and I would not fail
To buy one at a clearance sale.
I'm smarter than your average cat;
Likely you already know that.
Indeed, it's true, matter of fact,
I carry a lot under my hat.
On IQ tests I'm off the scale,
So bright, I say, "Who needs a tail?"

VI.
Feline Troubles

An Incorrigible Cat

Once there was a chubby rat,
Neighbor to a tabby cat,
A cat so hungry and so thin
That all he was was bones and skin.

This scrawny cat with paws and claws
And whiskers white beside his jaws
Had teeth so sharp that when he bit
Rumor had it, that was it!

One dark day this hungry cat
By the hole of--guess who?-- sat.
He, a feline, feeling thinner
Hoped to catch that rat for dinner.

The tabby sought a quick success
And waited till it left its nest.
Out it scurried in a fright,
Into jaws cat snapped. Good night!

"Gulp! Gulp!" followed (forget bites)
"Help!" squeaked rat. "Turn on the lights!"
This rat was in a heap of trouble,
Wanting out and on the double!

The cat just smiled and licked his chops.
The perfect crime, no pesky cops!
Off he sauntered, time to sleep.
So long, rat! Goodbye, squeak!

The cat relaxed; he wasn't tense.
He'd swallowed all the evidence.
But somehow every crime gets out.
(The rats had ratted on the cat, no doubt!)

Headlines read, "Our Rat Is Dead!"
The sheriff puppy doggie said:
"I'll catch the cat who ate that Rat.
We'll have a trial and chew the fat."

Soon sheriff tracked cat up a tree.
He growled, "Cat, criminal, come with me
To appear before judge and rodent jury."
At that the cat began to worry.

Wasn't eating rats all right?
Didn't laws state "Might makes right?"
The tabby pled his criminal case
To twelve rats in the jury's place.

But the jury's laws knew better.
They dealt justice to the letter.
Swiftly was their verdict reached
And in that courtroom made this speech:

"Guilty! Guilty!" squeaked the jury,
"Guilty by the laws that be.
We, the jury, find the cat guilty.
Off to jail! Hurray! Yippee!"

"Woe is me!" the kitty yelled.
As suddenly his tummy swelled.
"Gas!" he cried. "It must be gas!
Poor me! Pour me tea, sassafras."

Then amazingly, as he sipped his tea,
Surprise! He burped and the rat popped free!
Out he came without a squeeze
And off he ran to eat some cheese.

How relieved the tabby felt,
(But still starved as he tightened up his belt.)
"Case dismissed!" the judge decreed.
"I must rule this tabby freed."

Up the jurors jumped to go.
Out they scampered in a row.
The tabby followed close behind.
Guess what he had on his mind!

Moral: Rat or cat, fat or thin,
Watch your step and save your skin.

The Neighborhood Cat Lady

Our neighbor keeps cats in her house
We can be sure without one mouse
And certain, too, beyond a doubt,
She must have twenty cats about.

We've noticed that her favorite cat
Has been well fed and now is fat
Behaving like a spoiled brat
Who only glared if he heard "Scat!"

How does this lady feed so many
Cats to see they all have plenty?
It's not a question we pursue
Though we're curious; are you, too?

And what does the cat lady herself eat
With so many kitties around her feet?
Tuna, no doubt, fillet of fish
Using her "I Love Kitties" dish.

Don't know about you, but certainly we
Find it more than a mystery
Why one woman wants all these cats
Is she quite herself or a little bats?

If a health official were to come
She'd get up her dander and think it dumb.
"I'm running a cat house," she'd likely say,
"I'm the meows' mom—now get away."

Then what, we wonder, would they do,
Fine the lady or pursue
Other actions much more dire?
Set a deadline, down to the wire?

Or serve a warrant for her arrest
Which would cause her great distress,
Not just to her, but every cat
Living in her habitat.

If a feline home were next to you,
What, we wonder, would *you* do?
Would you, could you let them be,
Back off, just say, "C'est la vie!"?

Yowly Alley Cats

What makes two roving alley cats
Get yowly in the night?
Are these poor things just hungry
Or reeling from a fight?

As they caterwaul awhile
Under the rising moon,
So shrill a sound the ruckus makes,
They cannot stop too soon.

Noise like this disturbs the sleep
Of neighbors all around,
Who, upset, cannot ignore
The shrieking yowly sound.

With decibels like these outside
They wish they'd go away,
Depart, retire, remove, be gone,
Anything but stay.

How to stop it? How to end it?
How prevent sleep loss?
Chase them off to end their sounds,
Find a shoe to toss.

What makes a pair of alley cats
Get yowly in the night?
Who knows? One can only hope
They'll end their raucous fight.

But this we know, at this late hour,
We wish them gone or fed,
Not making us toss and turn all night
Kept wide awake in bed.

Herding Wild Cats

Herding cats is hardly fun,
Although, in truth, it can be done.
In circuses one sees proof there
With five or six cats, though it's rare.
We're speaking here mostly of lions
And tigers, they must keep an eye on.
It isn't easy, that's for sure,
And certain keepers do prefer
To train these creatures into shape,
Make them mind and concentrate
On the task that lies before,
Even though they often roar.
It is a matter of professional pride
To keep them lioned up like bears, oh my!

Cat Lesson

Not all that glisters turns out gold *
Thomas Gray, the poet, told
Us in an ode about his cat
That sadly died, tried to get at

Two goldfish swimming in a tub,
Misstepped and drowned, alas, (glub, glub)
When would-be feline felon fell in, oh
It's quite a shame this way to go

Mewing, forsaken in the water,
Where fickle Fate, alas, had caught her
And had taken its cruel toll
On the tabby, whose sole goal

Was to catch two tasty fish,
Nothing more or less than this
That turned out was a foolish whim
Considering kitty could not swim,

And though she'd mewed and sought salvation,
None could be had on this occasion
By Neptune or what gods there are
In constellation stars afar

Who heard cat not, alack, alas,
Or else ignored her, took a pass
And let the little feline drown
(Really let the kitty down)

Which most would say was quite unfair,
Except to the goldfish (two were there),
Who, had they vocal cords and voice,
We know would more than twice rejoice

And say the cat had got his due,
Which makes a point to me and you
(Though never would we try to preach
Or beseech, but only teach)

By means of just this one-line speech:
"Be careful where you dare to reach!"

---

*The last three lines of "Ode on the Death of a Favourite Cat, Drowned in a Tub of Goldfishes" by Thomas Gray, 1716-1771, read as follows: "Not all that tempts your wandering eyes /And heedless hearts, is lawful prize; / Nor all that glisters gold."

Saving a Lady's Cat

Fire station's phone rings,
Lady in distress
Cries, "My cat's stranded
Up a tree. Gracious!"

"Please come, will you?
Not a moment to be spared.
Cat's up the neighbor's tree
And he's so scared!"

"What's your address, ma'am?
Be there right away.
No need to worry,
We'll save the day."

Fire truck arrives,
Lights going 'round,
Men with ladders
To coax kitty down.

Men get it done,
Put cat in lady's arms,
Much more fun
Than chasing fire alarms.

"Oh, thank you, firemen
For rescuing my cat,"
Croons the lady.
"Come in for tea and chat."

Poor little kitty,
Hear him purring,
Happy now,
No more worrying.

Lady puts cat down.
After all it's been through
Feeds it tuna
And fresh milk, too.

"Can't thank you enough
For saving my kitty
Out of those branches
Here in our city."

"Come in for cookies,
Please, won't you?
You're heroes, truly,
Your whole crew,

And have some tea;
It's the least I can do.
All's well that ends well,
Cat's safe, thank you."

"Don't mention it, ma'am.
It's what we do,
Rescuing cats,
A pleasure serving you,

"But gotta be going."
They get back in their truck,
Happy to be helpful.
"Thanks and good luck."

Start up the truck,
Saviors of the cat,
Drive off in a hurry,
Crush the cat flat!

---

*This story, an urban legend for decades, is well retold in the book by Robert Fulghum, *Words I Wish I Wrote* (Cliff Street Books: New York, 1997).

Cat Wouldn't Fiddle

Hey diddle-diddle,
Cat wouldn't fiddle,
Wouldn't fiddle a single note.
"Cat gut for string
Just isn't my thing,"
He cried, and that's a quote.

Cats of Ancient Egypt

In ancient Egypt, though it's odd,
Cats were worshipped as a god,
Which is to say, were deified,
Then buried after mummified
As a way to keep around
Their cadavers in the ground
Dry and carefully protected,
Though rarely afterward inspected.
Thousands of them in their day
Were kept preserved in this way.
Today we find them now and then
When a ton of sand has been
Carefully shoveled and brushed aside
To find them -- dead, but dignified.

Harbor Cat

A cat who drifted in like fog
On paws, alas, soon met a dog,
Or the reverse some insist,
And that is why today it's missed.

VII.
Wild Cat Tales

The Cheetah

It is a well-established fact
That the cheetah is the fastest cat,
All muscles, sinews, little fat,
Known to dash in no time flat.

Most animals around it fear
The cheetah might end their career,
Especially so for grazing deer
Unlucky to be far too near.

The wisest know to stay away,
Not let their lives be put in play
Lest they become the cheetah's prey,
Which is to say his next buffet.

To summarize this cat's career
With speed and grace, it would appear,
If there are deer that stray nearby,
Chances are that some will die.

So listen deer, if this is you,
Be extra careful what you do
In Africa, when you roam there
Near a cheetah, do beware!

The Cougar

The cougar, people claim, is fierce
From his tail clear to his ears,
And so elicits feline fears
Whenever this shy cat appears.
It has been years since one was seen,
Adult, a cub, or even teen,
Though we have heard one was demeaned,
His den-mate even called a fiend.
To say such things about a pair
Would not be kind, would not be fair.
Indeed, this kind of nomenclature
Insults their character and nature.
We should protect them--they are rare--
Respect their place in field and lair.

The Leopard

Across the veldt the leopard trots
Well camouflaged with lots of spots,
A cat intending to confront
Unwary deer for which he'll hunt,

A deer that's weak, perhaps one young,
Away from herd, far out among
The hinterlands, not staying near
Its stronger kind, with far less fear.

With these the leopard uses stealth.
He looks for prey that have poor health
Or maybe those with injury
To catch and drag high up a tree

Where he'll eat deer at his ease
Safely, slowly as 'twill please,
Satisfied to sleep, grow fat,
And be content, the leopard cat.

Lions cannot reach him there.
He knows this well, he's taken care
To keep his meal up high, away
From other predators who may

Wish to take what he has got,
Game they want, but they have not,
Prey he found they did not slay,
Prey for free, not have to pay.

The leopard, though, will have no part
Of thievery; he's far too smart.
In branches high he likes to be
To eat and sleep contentedly.

There he stays to yawn and laze,
Enjoy the view on many days.
He has his routine down, and pat,
This very clever leopard cat.

Save the Tyger

Tyger! Tyger! full of fight,
Hunter, stalker in the night,
Taking prey is your way,
While more endangered every day,

Graceful, cunning, how you hunt
With mighty muscles elegant,
Beautiful as cats can be
In your splendid symmetry.

"Save the tyger!" is our cry,
And we mean it; we will try,
Printed here in words of ink
Hoping you won't go extinct.

Tyger! Tyger! be aware
Many people really care
For your welfare and your fate,
Before you're gone and it's too late.

The Ocelot

You may have thought the ocelot,
As cats go, could do better
If he had been early taught
To always stick together,
Not go hunting all alone,
Especially at night,
Over territory roam
Rather than in light.
But who's to say or criticize?
That's just his way, foolish or wise.
He's still a cat at that and splendid,
Matter of fact, as nature intended.

The Jaguar

The jaguar, like a fancy car,
Is full of dash and jump and rharrr.
A real cool cat, it likes to hide
In jungles deep and stay inside.
The beauty of this splendid beast
Is for the eyes a lovely feast,
Although because it's solitaire,
To see it now is very rare.
Its range, once large, is shrinking fast
As time goes by and may not last.
Its friends are worried, for alas,
Survival tests it may not pass.
If driven from its habitat,
Here's the rundown: goodbye cat.

Afri-cats

The puissance of Afri-cats
Cannot be denied.
Watch them when they get in spats
And see their strength applied.
One quick bite to the throat
Can kill a wildebeest,
Done almost as if by rote
Leading to a feast.
Muscles are what they rely on;
Sinews help as well.
When you are a lady lion,
Clearly it can spell
An end to prey that won't take long;
One strong lion and they're gone.

The Polecat and Panther

The following questions need an answer:
How different are polecat and panther?
Are their sizes large or small
Compared to what, short or tall?

Will they answer if you call?
Are they a similar animal?
Would seeing either give one pause?
How compare their claws and jaws?

If put together side-by-side,
What differences could they not hide?
Would their hides (or pelts) both look the same,
Or is one wild, the other tame?

What would bring more clarity
To their differences or similarity?
If you're in a convenient position
To look up a dictionary definition

Of a polecat and a panther
And really want to have an answer,
By all means and with due speed
Turn to their pages, go and read!

The Liger

The liger is a mixed-up cat,
Merged genetically, in fact.
When lions and tigers meet each other
And mate, their cubs we soon discover
Share their traits half and half.
Really, folks! Try not to laugh.
The liger has some lion mane
And muted stripes, not lion plain.
I'm telling you, it's really true.
A few are even at the zoo
Where they watch us watchers gawk
While pacing they frown at our talk
As if to say, "Hey, what's the deal?
Quit staring—can't you see we're real?"

Paw note:

One wonders what would William Blake
Of this combo kitty make.
Would he say they burned as bright
As tigers in forests of the night?

VIII.
Bow-wow, Meow, and Moo*

---

*"Moo?" How, you might ask, did moo-cows sneak into this book of poems mainly about cats? Well, cows are cattle, after all. And the dogs? By dogged determination.

Bow-wow, Meow, and Moo

A big bow-wow and small meow
Hungry to be fed
Waited for their kitchen chow,
Then ambled off to bed, to bed,
Then ambled off to bed.

Into dreams bowwow was swept,
The meow followed soon.
And while they slept, they dreamed cows leapt
Over the harvest moon, the moon,
Over the harvest moon.

But can a cow jump quite *that* high
To reach a cheesy moon,
Go ahead and really fly
In mid-July or June, in June,
In mid-July or June,

Make a run like that for fun,
And hear a "tick-tick-tocket,"
Clocks count down from ten to one,
Then blast-off like a rocket,
Then blast-off like a rocket?

Yes, up they went with a mighty roar
A million miles or more,
To reach a blue cheese moon, to soar
And land on legs, yes, cow legs four,
To land on cow legs four.

The bow-wow doesn't know this though,
He thinks it's just a dream.
The cat (meow), purrs thus and so,
Unaware of this 'twould seem, 'twould seem,
Unaware of this 'twould seem.

Whereas by now the cows (and how!)
Are munching gouda cheese
Wide awake, make no mistake,
As much cheese as they please, they please,
As much cheese as they please.

It has not dawned on those below
The cows have left for good,
Though farmers are supposed to know
No cows can fly nor should, nor should,
No cows can fly nor should.

But many, many years ago,
When butter was the favored spread,
More than margarine (oleo),
Cows flew or so it's said, it's said,
Cows flew or so it's said.

Then we'd have heard and even seen
Cows mooing on the moon
Loud enough to hear, I mean,
Making a moody tune, a tune,
Making a moody tune:

"Moo-moo-moo!
Moo-moo-moo!"
Town folk and farmers, too,
Knew this was really true, was true,
Knew this was really true.

So even now when dogs bow-wow
And hungry cats meow,
Some people say it is because
They maybe hear a cow, a cow,
They maybe hear a cow.

We might allow this as a fact.
And some would testify
That since a dog and cat will act
This way, then cows must fly, must fly,
This way, then cows must fly.

And who are we and who am I
To say it isn't true,
That long ago moo-cows could fly
And maybe some still do, still do,
And maybe some still do?

A Parakeet and a Cat

A parakeet was singing,
Swinging in her cage.
A cat was nearby watching,
Hungry, too, we'll wage.

"Let me at that bird," said he,
Muttering to himself.
"She looks delicious, and maybe
I'll eat her in good health."

The clever parakeet, however,
Had rather different plans,
Dreams and flights of fancy
To distant tropic lands.

"If only I could fly there,"
The parakeet declared,
"But then I'd leave my cage here
And that would make me scared

"Since flying isn't easy,
Not with my short clipped wings.
I fear the cat would seize me
If I left my cage and swings.

"I know the cat is waiting;
He hardly is my friend.
Were I to fly, he'd catch me
And that would be my end."

So the parakeet kept swinging
And chirping on her perch,
Keeping calm by singing
As if she were in church.

A soloist, she sang,
And twittered on alone,
Never flew the coop,
Stayed in her safety zone.

The cat, of course, knew nothing
Of her musings, none he heard,
But licked his paws, complaining
Of warbling by the bird,

And so that day went hungry,
Acknowledged his defeat,
Every which way from Sunday
With no parakeet to eat!

The Two-tailed Tomcat

We knew a Tomcat (this is true),
Who had instead of one tail, two,
And one was left, the other right,
Which kept him warm curled up at night.
And during the day he used to play
With both his tails and straight away
He'd chase them round his back a lot
And pounce on each till both were caught.
Then he'd preen each one in turn,
Clean them both, a great concern,
Let them dry a little while,
And fluff them up, which made him smile.
All this is what he liked to do
That tomcat with two tails we knew.

Chary Birds

With cats around, most birds act chary,
And have good cause, cause to worry.
Paws and claws and jaws nearby
Will be watching where they fly,
Patient, stealthy, quick to spring
At all feathery things that sing.
Cats, of course, find hunting fun,
Especially when successfully done.
Birds, we venture, don't agree
As they look on warily
Since feline motives are suspect
And birds will pick apart and peck
At what cat aspirations are:
To eat them like they're caviar.

Not Real News

What are we, folks, to make of it
That once there was a man who bit
A gentle, harmless, helpless dog
After drinking too much grog?
The papers all declared it news
(Reporters write whate'er they choose)
But if a dog should bite a man,
You'd find the story rarely ran,
For what would be the news in this?
It's one most papers would dismiss
And even rabid dogs don't often
These days put folks in a coffin.
So when a dog bites man today
It's not real news reporters say.

Hark, the Bark!

Consider how a dog says "Hark!"
It's not a casual remark,
Rather every "Bark! Bark! Bark!"
Whether home or in a park

Means he thinks there's something wrong,
He's worried with what's going on.
Your dog is feeling apprehension,
And he wants your full attention.

It might mean, "Look, danger there!"
Or he sees a squirrel or hare
Has made a sudden guest appearance,
For your dog a fun experience.

He wants to pull you on his leash,
Tries to run and hopes to reach
Whatever critter he has seen,
That is what his barking means!

Thin Dog, Fat Cat

Our dog is thin, our cat is fat.
We've gathered how they got to that
Difference, we mean in size.
We have our hunch and theorize
One took his time before he ate,
The other couldn't or wouldn't wait.
Thus one grew great, the other thin,
And now these are the shapes they're in.
Their eating habits were not wise
And so it came as no surprise.
What happened is by inference
The reason for their difference.
The cat grew huge, the dog stayed small;
One fast, one slow explains it all.

Better Dog Days Done

What's a dog to do when he
Has seen a better day,
Turn his bones in docilely,
Leave his house and stray?

Bark awhile, lick his dish,
Growl, "I won't obey
Anything my owners wish
No matter what they say?"

Bowwow his head? Go to bed?
Look the other way?
Whimper, curl up and play dead?
Sleep away the day?

Not give a yip? Bark, "So long?"
Refuse to be on guard?
Arf no more, leave, be gone,
Not stick around the yard?

What's a dog to do when he
Has lost his smell and sight
Except protest deliberately:
"I won't go gentle into night;
I'll rage and fight and bite!"?

But if there is a place somewhere,
A doggie heaven in space,
He might leave here and go to there
Where rabbits run, he'll chase.

Tale of Caution

I knew a dog who bit a man
By accident on the hand,
Not expected, wasn't planned
When the dog and man began
Playing games of toss and fetch,
Throwing balls the dog would catch,
Just a common thing to do
As the man and dog both knew,
Until the dog grew too excited
And the game, alas, invited
Things to go a bit too far,
To bite, then stitches and a scar.
Yet, know when shove turns into push,
One bite on the hand beats two in the tush.

IX.
Doggie Tales

A Dog's Concerns

A dog's concern is foremost food,
Next play and exercise.
A place to sleep is also good,
While petting, too, applies.
His owner does his best and tries
To give a dog a home,
Comfortable and of a size
That leaves him free to roam,
A place conducive to his health,
Plus veterinary care
With affection and a wealth
Of attention, lots to spare.
With all these things a dog will be
Friendly and live happily.

A Puppy's Way

What's a puppy supposed to do
But chew a shoe, I ask you,
And anything else
Found 'round your house
When it's just brand new?

How adorable pups are; they
Romp about, run and play.
From the start
They'll capture your heart
In a happy doggie way.

Later they will learn to stay,
Heel, roll over, sit, obey,
And because you care, your puppy
Soon will sense it's truly lucky
There to warm your day.

My Wiener Dog

What makes a wiener dog so long
And low down to the ground?
Why does he yip? Is that his song?
I love to hear that sound,
Also to see him romp and run
And move his wiggly rump
As he heads downstairs; it's fun
To see his belly bump.
My wiener dog's adorable,
As cute as he can be,
And it would be a tragedy
If he were lost to me.
And I shall never give him up;
He's family, my wiener pup.

Puppy Fears

Our puppy fears a thunderclap,
Supposing it's a sky attack,
Runs and hides beneath our bed,
Lies there still and hides his head.
We try to calm him; it's no use.
He fears the likes of Thor or Zeus.
"Help!" he whimpers, his remark
Frantically, or "Bark! Bark! Bark!"
Or if hail storm comes, he'll scare
And cower, poor thing, lie in terror.
Doesn't matter what we say;
Under bed he plans to stay.
Only later he's coaxed out
When his safety's not in doubt.

My Dog, Ben

I have a dog named Ben,
He is my fondest friend.
I walk him every day,
But he has run away.

I hope he's found; he may
Be picked up as a stray.
His collar has his name
And address, but all the same

I hope he's found and soon,
Perhaps this afternoon.
I'd like to have him home;
I wish he wouldn't roam.

I do not know quite why
He ran away, but I
Will keep a closer eye
On him next time or try.

He still has much to learn.
I'll ask on his return,
Say to him right then,
"Ben, where have you been?"

Then likely he will say
In his wiggly-waggy way,
"I didn't mean to stray,
I just ran off to play."

What Dogs Do

Friendly dogs wag their tails,
Come when they are called.
Some do tricks, fetch thrown sticks
And may retrieve a ball.

If a dog barks, stay away!
They are warning you.
Dogs like this don't want to play
And dangerous ones pursue.

Bark, bite, lick and sit,
That's what dogs can do,
Ruff, come, roll over, run,
These behaviors, too.

Every dog is different, so
Here's a good suggestion:
When you meet a dog that's new,
Be cautious, use discretion.

Red

The dog we had, we called her Red,
A miniature dachshund (quadruped)
And red she was from tail to head;
Oh, what a happy life she led!

The way she walked was with a wiggle,
Funny so it made us giggle.
Head to tail, between her middle,
When she ran, she'd rather wriggle.

Especially through grass when long,
She'd disappear, nearly gone,
Except for tail, but just its tip;
Oh, she was cute, our little pip.

And cuddly, too, a friend was she,
As much as any dog could be.
We loved that dog, our little Red,
Sure miss her and the life she led.

No Good Goodbye

It's been some years since our dog died,
Nikita was her name.
And though we had to let her go
She comes back all the same.

While we have tried, tried to forget,
Our love remembers still
Her happy, jaunty stride, our walks,
Forget—we never will.

Though we complained and grumbled some
To walk her in the cold,
The freezing bite of wind at night
Let her delight unfold.

Her warmth, her joy, her wagging tail,
Her pleasure as we ran,
Her leaping gait in deepest snow--
Forget? We never can.

She pranced, she bounded like a pup,
She skipped along with pleasure.
What moments like that meant to us
No words can ever measure.

Farewell, dear pup, Siberian soul,
So friendly, warm and furry,
Our memories so fond of you
Won't fade in any hurry.

Our loss of you is all too real
To ever go away.
Nikita, in our hearts we feel
Love for you to this day.

Forget our feelings? Not a chance.
Deny? Why even try?
You meant more than we even knew.
We know no good goodbye.

Walk the Dog

"Walk the dog—it'll do you good,"
My mother would say. She understood
A little exercise each day
For us would go a long, long way.

Our dog required it—so did I
Most of the time, and that is why
To this day I walk the dog.
Many are the miles we've logged,

Thousands it must be by now
As busy days and life allow.
Both dog and I are better for it,
Free from extra weight—why store it?

Yes, I could go to a gym,
But why? I'd rather go with him,
Walk my dog. It gives us joy,
Doesn't it, pooch? Come on boy!

About the Author

Jeffry Glover, winner of a Robert Frost Foundation national poetry award and a leader in education award, creates delightful tales in verse for all ages. His collections of rhyming stories are in turn whimsical, humorous, heartwarming, serious, and just plain fun. His newest books include *The Wildebeest and a Bunch of Crock* and *Letter to a Dandelion: Earth Verse for Gardeners and Nature Lovers*, now available or available soon! Visit Jeff's website to check out more of his books at *www.JeffryGlover.com*. Scan below to reach Jeff's website!

www.ingramcontent.com/pod-product-compliance
Lightning Source LLC
Chambersburg PA
CBHW030054100526
44591CB00008B/149